AF576941

Something Knows the Moment

Poems by

Scott Owens

Main Street Rag Publishing Company
Charlotte, North Carolina

Cover art: Clayton Joe Young
Author photo by: Jessie Carty

Library of Congress Control Number: 2011923732

ISBN: 978-1-59948-302-3

Produced in the United States of America

Main Street Rag
PO Box 690100
Charlotte, NC 28227
www.MainStreetRag.com

For Tim Peeler, Steven Sherrill, Ann Carver,
Hepzhibah Roskelly, Carolyn Thomas,
and all the others who made me think about it.

ACKNOWLEDGMENTS

Grateful acknowledgment is due the editors of the following journals in which some of these poems were previously published:

Asheville Poetry Review: "Eve Descending"
Blue Fifth Review: "In Splintered View of God"
Blue Unicorn: "In the Cathedral of Fallen Trees"
Charlotte Poetry Review: "God, Creating the Birds, Envisions Adam," "Post Mortem"
Cream City Review: "St. Sebastian's Widow"
Future Earth Magazine: "Prelapse"
Georgia Journal for "Remembering Walking;"
Grasslimb: "Trajectory"
Gutter Eloquence: "Through the Valley of the Shadow"
Heavy Bear: "Meat Jesus;"
Imagining Heaven: "Clarence;"
Innisfree Poetry Review: "Leap of Faith," "Resistance"
Iodine Poetry Journal: "The Dying Cost of Rising"
JMWW: "Another Making"
Kakalak: "By-Product"
*ken*again*: "The Art of War"
Laurel Review: "Returning to the Father"
Leaf Garden: "Insufficient Knowledge"
Main Street Rag: "Refusing Grace"
Mind in Motion: "The Stars Are Far Away and Blind"
Muddy River Poetry Review: "Sense of Place"
Orange Room Review: "Naming God"
Pig in a Poke: "The Boy in the Chair Finds Christ"
Pirene's Fountain: "Deficit," "Father's House," "The Imperfect Garden"
Polu Texni: "Instructions at the Gate"
Prime Decimals: "Absolute Value"
protestpoems.org: "Using My Name in Vain"
Rusty Truck: "Leaving Eden"
Scythe: "After the Flood"
Side Stream: "Nearing the end of my sentence"
The Smoking Poet: "Having His Hands Before Him"
The Sow's Ear: "Original Sin"
Tar River Poetry: "The Arrival of Wings"
Tertulia: "Misguided Angel," "Now Hiring Holy Angels"
Town Creek Poetry: "The Dream of St. Francis"
Untitled Country: "Nomenclature"
Waterways: "The Passion"
Wild Goose Poetry Review: "The Sensual World"
Willows Wept Review: "The Journey"

Some of these poems appeared in a limited edition chapbook of poems entitled *The Persistence of Faith* from Sandstone Press in 1995.

CONTENTS

ACTS OF CREATION

THE LIVES OF THE SAINTS AND OTHERS

THE ANGELS' NIGHT OFF

THE PERSISTENCE OF FAITH

WHAT TO MAKE OF A RUINED THING

ACTS OF CREATION

in the beginning
God could think of nothing
better than this

HAVING HIS HANDS BEFORE HIM

"Less than All cannot satisfy Man"
—William Blake

Having his hands before him
having his arms and shoulders needing work
having his mouth and eyes, feet and loins
and something called the void
God wanted more
so with his big right foot
he split the sky in half
so with the heel of his hand
he shaped the day into light and dark
so with great globules of spit
he hung the sun and moon
pissed the stars across the sky
coughed out clouds
threw down trees and vines
and bushes and grasses
and even a shrub or two.

Still, having his hands before him
his forehead shining
his hair hanging about his face
having his ears and nose and high cheekbones
he wanted more
so with his white teeth
he chewed up bits of earth
and molded tiger and lamb
dove and whale, serpent and flea
so with his toes
he scratched out a garden
so with his mirror
he chiseled a pair of little gods
so with his mouth

he said, "Be fruitful and multiply
but keep your hands off my tree."

Then, having his hands before him,
having his mirror cracked
his eyebrows knitted together
his lips pursed inward
having his teeth dripping
and his fruit spoiled
he wanted more
so with his eyes
he cried a flood
so with his breath
he blew up wind
to knock down towers and walls
so with his tongue
he burned a bush
and etched in stone
and lapped the center of the sea.

Having his hands before him
his fingers plucking his skin
having his chest bared
his belly grown round
his buttocks pushing out
he wanted more
so with his pelvis
he had a son
so with his silence
he nailed him to a tree
so with the shadow of his hand
he took him back
and with his long spine

he lay down beside him
and wept deep
into the hands before him.

RESISTING CREATION

It was only chaos of course because it wasn't his,
like any house you walk into and immediately want to change.
Like him it had always been there. And he had grown tired
of it touching him in its own way, turning out the lights
when he wasn't looking, flipflopping heaven and earth
on a whim, constantly changing one thing to another.

He wanted to start from scratch, to recreate life
in his own image, lined, ruled, perfectly squared.
He wanted to make the universe like a diagram,
each thing pigeonholed neatly beneath another.

So finally with one atomic finger he leveled it all
into nothing, or rather into a mountain of glowing compost
he could dish out as he saw fit. He laid down a framework
of order, subjected night to day, earth to heaven,
everything to himself, made the sun as many times larger
than the moon as it is farther away from the earth.

"Believe," he told them, "that I am the one.
Follow my law and none other. Be happy
to have this purpose of praising what I am."

But at night, in the dark, it moved again the way it wanted,
slithered across the lines he'd drawn, became fruitful
and multiplied in all the wrong ways, mixing race,
gender, species, leaving its gooey mess of creation
on his doorstep, window, every wall he'd made.

So of course he grew tired of it again, tried to give it
one enormous bath to wash away the bits of life popping up
everywhere. But even before the waters receded it danced
on top of the waves, gathered enough silt to make a mountain,
grew lanterns to see beneath the murky deep.

So finally he said, "Fuck it. Here's a boy to play with.
Let him watch you for a while." And of course it consumed
the boy in no time, left him hanging cold on a tree,
and God, dejected and alone, retired, waiting
on the other side of darkness with his black book,
his fiery lake, an enormous chip on his shoulder.

MOTHER OF INVENTION

The origin of origin is O
as in, O, my God, (if I can call
him mine when I've shown time
and time again so little faith
or use for what he may or may
not be) what have you done
or worse left undone
for those like me to do
on somewhat less than
ten percent of my already less than
brain sometimes coming out okay
despite inadequacy—love and sharing
and taking care to keep things green—
and sometimes coming out wrong—
greed and impatience and never
having enough of anything—
and mostly coming out in ways
we couldn't begin to understand—
progress, fairness, foresight
that couldn't help but be missing from
the making of rows beside a river,
the making of homes beside the rows,
the making of streets among the homes
that lead to this town I come from,
this hill outside the town I come from,
this farm on the hill outside the town I come from,
these people on the farm on the hill outside of the town I come from,
this O they believe in, the perfect circle,
the unclosing eye, the unrelenting zero
that leaves them hopefully unprepared.

THE IMPERFECT GARDEN

There are things he never wanted this way,
things he never planned, the slip of hand
stretching the nose into elephant, neck
into giraffe, lost legs leaving the snake
on its belly, the nightmare springing into lion,
his own uncareful eye leading
to aardvark, manatee, pelican.

He thought that using his own body as model
he could do no wrong, but mistakes were made.
When he grew tired he lost his concentration.
Some were born deformed, others given bodies
too large or small, wings they couldn't use,
shells they couldn't escape from.
Many were simply left unfinished.

He knew he could fix them, if he wanted,
make them just the way he sketched them out,
each one perfect and beautiful, but always
there was something in the way they walked,
talked, moved about without a backward glance,
without a care for him that made him say
this is life now, you can do nothing to stop it.

GOD, CREATING THE BIRDS, ENVISIONS ADAM

Detail from the North Porch of Chartres Cathedral

No feathers, no fins. Each thing he wanted
to outdo the last. How now could he
surpass these flowers of the air, his mind
already tired, his hands sore, his body
spent from shaping. Nothing less than himself
would do, he thought. His own image
in miniature, puppet, mannequin, mirror
that moves. Important now to forget the early
mistakes, jellyfish, plankton, platypus,
to focus on this final act of creation.

In the darkness he saved from his own
restless hands he drank the wine he'd created,
his only company the quiet angels of his mind,
yes-men with halos and swords.
He will have no wings. That night
he slept the troubled sleep of dreams.
He saw faces that mocked his own,
fingers that picked his skin apart,
mouths that spat in the hands that made them.
His teeth will be like white soldiers, angry and hard.

Early the next day, his eyes barely open,
his head still humming from the night before,
he scraped the flesh from his own face,
opened a mouth, pressed his thumb hard
into the wells of eyes, pulled up ears
and nose, stretched out torso, arms, legs,
fingers, toes. He worked for hours shaping
the supple curve of back, rounding the buttocks,
pinching the tight cup of prick and balls.
His hands will be like these, clumsy and precise.

At last he draped it over the white sticks
he cherished, measured out sinew and nerve,
vein and gut, planted the bright seed
of his favorite tree in the loam of brain,
stood back, looked, retched,
dredged the life again from his lungs,
spat it into the mouth, called it
man, son of God, keeper of earth,
dropped it headfirst, naked, crying,
bruised and bloody to the ground.

BEST OF DAYS

God, like all of us, was at his best
on Tuesday, or whatever he called the second
day of work. *Keep it simple*,
he must have said after Monday's overreaching,
light and dark, heaven and earth.
Simple separation now
before things get messy,
an impenetrable wall separating our world
from his. And it was all downhill
from there, like any work week would be,
Wednesday's land and sea marred
with desert and earthquake, typhoon and tidal wave,
Thursday's sun and moon with supernovas,
the barren sea of tranquility,
Friday with dodo and lamprey, hagfish
and buzzard. By Saturday, of course,
he couldn't have cared less, distracted
by waiting for that night's carousing,
the next day's sleeping in.

THE FIFTH DAY

On the first day there was only the sound
of his own making, a noise as quiet as thought.
On the second day he heard for the first time
the earth crackling with heat, the water
moving, the wheels of the sky turning,
and the dull silence beside him.
On the third day he heard the sun
unfolding a flower, the vines creeping
across the earth, leaves outstretching,
wind shaking limbs together.

Yesterday sang all night in his ears,
warbled like light across his mind,
rattled his eyes open,
touched his lips, still without a sound.

Today, there is speaking,
there is crying,
there is howling at the moon
he threw out like a spare part.
There are the many-voweled voices
of animals calling each other by name.

Tomorrow he will learn what his own
tongue could do if he would let it,
if he would give himself just one person
to talk to, one person to talk to him
without saying yessir, nosir, amen.

BY-PRODUCT

Having made light,
he scattered what was left
across the face of stars and moons.

Having finished with planets,
he spread the extra rock in a belt
between Jupiter and Mars.

Having created water,
he gathered the remains
in buckets of clouds.

Having made mountains and fields,
he swept what was left
into piles called dunes or desert.

There was always waste,
corollary of creation,
weeds, ash, dust.

He called the excess darkness,
eclipse, the extra time, leap year,
the unused green stuff, kudzu.

Being done with animals,
he kept an ectoplasmic pool
of ooze he'd call evolution.

Having finished with man,
he couldn't tell the difference
between the created and the waste,

gave breath to each
and sent them on their way
to see what they might make.

THEOPHANY

No matter how I tried
I couldn't stop myself
from watching you.
I couldn't stop myself
from thinking you, dreaming you
divine, defined, deified, denied.
My god, who could think themselves
able to wrap their mind
around such a concept?
Who would dare imagine
such a face, conceive
such hands as these,
see these thighs,
seize these thighs
as the kneeling bench,
tongue become prayer
praying for absolution
praying for communion
praying for the body
for the blood
for the body
for the blood
for the body
for the blood
to come into them.
Forgive us.
We know not.

INSUFFICIENT KNOWLEDGE

So we decided to no longer be victimized by chance,
 though we had little luck in doing so.
So we decided there must be reasons for the way things were,
 though wherever we looked they escaped us.
So we decided there must be meaning to the effort, something more
 than this, though it seemed tenuous at best.
So we decided to make a god to explain it all,
 though we didn't know how.
So we decided to make him like us,
 though we knew he would have to be better.
So we decided to place him in the sky, give him lasting breath, wide-
 ranging vision, a strong hand, though that left little for us.
So we decided to bring him down to Earth,
 though we thought anything human couldn't be eternal.
So we hung him on a tree and sent him back to the sky and said wait
 there until we get this right, though we had no idea how long
 it might take.
So we decided to keep trying, worshipping an idea we can't understand
 but know to be vital to make.

NAMING GOD

To Norman, God was a storm.
What else could he be?
He had seen the storm, after all,
lift the roof off the barn
and plant it sideways, almost whole,
against the stand of scraggly pines
in the corner of the pasture
two hundred yards away.
He had seen it roll cars
two, three, four times
across the fields
in some kind of crazy race
where wheels didn't matter.
He had seen it topple trees
he knew to be stout enough
to hold himself, three brothers,
just as many cousins,
all at the same time,
not to mention sticks,
rocks, shields of oak
barrel lids and anything else
they carried with them into war.
And through it all he had heard
the old woman, louder
than the storm, naming, *God,*
help us! God, protect us!
God, don't take my babies!

ANOTHER MAKING

Tell me what you remember.
Nothing.
What did you feel?
Nothing.
C'mon, what did you feel?
Nothing, I said.
Nervous?
Perfectly normal.
Fear?
There's no right answer.
They picked on me.
Why?
My flesh was swollen.
I was too old. I was out of touch.
They said I was too demanding.
They wanted someone more like them.
Who were they?
My father, my wife, my landlord,
my boss, a stalker, a voyeur.
Why were they there?
They've always been there.
And then?
A lot of axes.
The sounds of breaking.
I was bigger than them.
They ran from me.
And then?
Nothing. They were all gone.
Silence.
Nothing?
Darkness.
Is that it?
I started over.

I made some light.
I made some shapes
for the light to touch.
The shapes made shadows.
Where the light touched them
the shapes made colors,
each color a little different from the next,
some colors even I couldn't see.
What else?
Cold air.
Snow and ice.
Storms.
Rivers and streams.
Water flowing downhill,
a waterfall.
Animals and trees.
Some animals that eat the trees,
some that eat themselves.
A bird or two,
one that rises
from its own ashes.
Iron and steel.
And then?
Things that moved on their own.
Things that made sounds at each other.
I thought it would be nice to have people.
Like who?
My father, my wife, a voyeur.

FOR THOSE CREATED WHOLE

Even in the beginning, they were few,
Adam and Athena, God, one must assume,
Plato's lovers, prototype of every beast,
else, how would they survive
the first of days with no tit
to suck, no drowze of fur to keep
them warm, no hand to hold, not even
a mother's tongue to lick the water away.
One has to wonder at the absence of those
formative years, Eve born bleeding,
Adam hunching after her, no knowledge
of seed or fish, word or moderation. Still,
it's impossible to imagine God the infant, hungry,
incontinent, unanswered tears watering the void.

MOTHER WHICH ART

Mother, who made me?

Why, I did, my child.

How, mother?

Out of my own flesh and blood I made you.
I fed you bread of my own body,
blood of my veins,
loved you towards your first breath,
carried you like the part of me you will always be.

Where, mother? Where did you make me?

Here, inside me. You lay inside me
until roses bloomed in your cheeks.
You moved like a leaf unfurling, stretching
your arms and legs, opening yourself
to all the light I offered,
then opening my own soft petals
to wake to both our crying.

Make another, like me, another child from inside you.

No, child. For that I would need to make a father first.

Who, mother? Who was my father?

A god, a force of nature, a substance
of my own creation, of my own mind's
needing, a swan, a bull, a shower
from heaven, a serpent, a flea,
a crow, a wolf, a bear,
a mirror with your face,
almost anything I want him to be.

LEARNING THE NAMES

Imagine Adam discovering the names
of every living thing for the first
time, crying out every beast
in the field, calling the red leaves
maple, the ever green pine,
announcing bergamot and burdock,
waxwing and shrike, iris and owl
without reason or rhyme but just
the joy of weight on his tongue.

Imagine Noah inviting them
into his ark by twos, renaming
the ones he never knew, calling
the horned ones rhino, the long
bird anhinga, the bright snake coral,
the one that never moves mantis.

Remember how you named things
the first time, releasing the roll
of vowels in your mouth, spitting out
sounds your body knew before you,
your lips unloosening bird, barking out
dog, counting sheep, dropping
tiger from the roof of your mouth,
sibillizing your way to snake.

Later, discovering consonants, you renamed
things, better, but still without right
or wrong, discovering the well-made
words that framed in mouth's shape
what the hands held, the perfect names
of things like breast, song, yes.

NOMENCLATURE

Adam used the easy adjectives
or none at all. The manatee
he left as manatee; the whale
he called blue. It was Eve
who saw to the heart of things,
heard the dove's mourning,
called the spider, recluse,
noticed the muteness of swans.
Old Moses left that part out.
Only one with knowledge
of forbidden fruit, familiar
with life as other, could imagine
those called hellbender and hellgrammite,
nightcrawler or man-of-war.

GOOD DAYS AND BAD

Even God had them. Living in the Void
it was inevitable.
Clementines and cherries. Lucifer and snot.
Loneliness
of the albatross.
October. Leaf mold.
Patience the lack of it.
Laughter or laughter.

Trees coated in ice. Religion.
Coffee. Duplicity.
Indian summers. Old age.
Language and pity. Disappointment and self-doubt.

The hopeless
romantic.
The urge to perversion.
The attraction of opposites.
Water. Suspicion.
The sound of walking through leaves.

Self-sacrifice. Deciding for others.
Mercy. Regret.
A cool evening when the work is done,
a light breeze is blowing, and the sun
sits on the horizon like something you've earned. Less
than perfect
vision. Hind sight.
Second chances.

THE LIVES OF THE SAINTS AND OTHERS

REMEMBERING WALKING

That was before God came down
and dropped his half-baked figures
in the garden, before Adam and Eve
were evicted for knowing how perfect
the shape of snake and grass go together.
That was when the miles were shorter,
the hills easier to climb,
when I could listen to my feet
scratching through dry grass, scraping
wet rocks, trampling the earth I owned,
when I still worried about stones
lodging between the pink pads of toes.

I remember walking
and do not miss it.
No one else hugs the earth
like I do,
wrapping body and soul around
the quiet curve of land. No one else
knows the measure of every grain
of sand they pass over. No one else
can know the scaly skin of pines,
twisted burl of oak, slick
puddle of plums changing into earth
like brothers.

PRELAPSE

Naked without knowing nakedness,
breasts nothing but breasts,
biological urge simply
something to do when bored
with nuts and berries,
inconsequential mastication of fruit.

Equal that day they lay together,
Eve touching herself
for nothing but pleasure,
laughing at Adam's hard on,
no knowledge of shame or power,
or a world where one must rule the other.

LIKELY STORY

It hardly seems possible the first sin
was eating an apple or feeling shame,
covering breast and crotch with foliage,
even rapping a stone against a brother's head.
I mean in a world where such beauty
abounds, and such appetite,
surely some sweeter seduction
must have come slithering along first
to lead Adam to forego promises,
covet, cheat, steal,
lie down in greener pastures.

EVE DESCENDING

The tree's secret was how not
to live invisibly, to be more
than wind, transparence of water,
worm sucking at the center of the rose,
hand holding the sky in place.

Eve descending saw how the willow
wept, the cherry blazed, the apple
kept its heart hidden, heard
the dove's cry and called it mourning,
felt the hawk's shadow above her,

the earth sucking at her feet,
the sun burning its mark in her back.
She touched her right hand, the bed
of her stomach, the blood between her legs,
walked with the soft sway of wanting.

What else was there? The invisibility
of everything except God?
Who would want to be an angel
that way, mute, beautiful,
stupidly happy bearing cups?

KNOWLEDGE OF GOOD

He could've, should've defended her,
pointed out the rules were unclear,
unfair, only delivered to him,
argued the serpent was subtle, unnatural,
and it all smacked of entrapment,
questioned why put the thing there
to begin with if he didn't want it so,
what was to be gained but loss.
He might've lied, said who'd want
to look at that all day anyway,
cock and balls, burning bush.
She would've done so for him,
carrying his sin inside, concealing,
nurturing, giving it room to grow.

FATHER'S HOUSE

The garden was his father's place.
Though he said he'd left it for him,
he'd never leave it completely,
dropping in whenever he wanted,
unannounced, demanding things
be kept as they were, exclaiming about
the trees, tssking his way to shame.

When things didn't go how he wanted,
he used the tricks of the old gods,
inducing sleep, performing
minor surgery, dictating labor.

Departure was inevitable,
the father never taking responsibility
for the mess he made, the pet
snake, ambitious girl, unwillingness
to share power or control.
A man and his father can never
live in the same house for long.

LEAVING EDEN

Being awake and alive
She spoke the meanings of flowers,
She said the birds held thoughts in their mouths.
Being new
She pressed her face against the windows,
Imagined paths unwinding before her.
Being young
She lay down on the rocks
Hung her feet in the stream.
Being kissed by the wind,
Being under the sky and stars
She rolled over, she said the trees
Bore heaven in their arms,
She said the weight was sometimes too much.

Being with him
She said her hands smelled of living,
She said things had to get better.
Being in pain she cried.
Being alone
She spoke of night's ejaculation of stars.
Being amazed
She said the darkness breathed dreams in her ears,
She said the sky was full of holes,
She said she almost saw through them.
Being the spoken, being named,
Being always the spoken to,
She wandered off to tracks behind the house,
Caught the metal fish-tail leaving town,
Screamed against the wheel's turning,
Never looked back, spoke her name
Into night's incessant unfolding.

ORIGINAL SIN

The sun was bright that day,
burning the skin of my arms,
my uncovered head, burning
the necks of grain I cut.

My brother sat in the shade
cutting the hair and throats
of lamb, letting their blood
drain into the ground, piling

their fat on altars to burn.
Why should he be favored?
What sacrifice made he?
The sun was bright that day

in a time of killing, when men
were marked for safe-keeping.
And I was a child of the times,
son of my mother, father

of sin. I heard the blood
of brothers crying out
from the ground, heard
the heat of the day moaning

in my head. I rose up
from the rows, the seed of earth
in my hand. I was the elder
son, returning to the land

the life taken from it.
I became the father of choice,
explorer of sin and other
dark places. I opened

my brother's body as I opened
the land to plant this seed
of knowing. I was the third
to be driven, to demand

the knowledge of men and women.
I could not be the Lord's
shepherd, destined to shepherd
the earth, move where it needed.

I could not live my brother's
life of unasking grace.
I was his lover, his slayer.
I became what keeps him alive.

AFTER THE FLOOD

When the waters receded,
when he parted them into Pacific and Atlantic,
when he looked down and saw the whole history
of human waste, a patchwork laid tip to toe,
side by side across the ground
like a single bloated skin,
what did he do?

Did he cry out?
Did he look at his own hands in terror?
Did he think genocide, infanticide, holocaust?
Did he see it was good
and dip his fingers into the blood
and excrement and write across the sky
in rainbow colors, *Not In My House*?

BETWEEN THE EARTH AND ME

"I do set my bow in the cloud and it shall be for a token of a covenant between me and the Earth."

Genesis 9:13

Misunderstood to imply man,
as so often ego leads us to do,
reading the poem as about us,
the overheard word, even the prophecy,
meaning only what was actually said,
contract whose terms are clearly stated:
the waters shall no more become
a flood to destroy all flesh.
The rest imagination, vain
optimism, mere interpretation.

COVENANT

When God said,
Like the stars in the sky,
Did he mean numbers only,
or did he intend scattered,
distant, lifeless, old,
mere image of what has
been gone for a lifetime,
source of dim light
lost among mortal ambience,
not quite eternal,
not quite relevant,
horribly misunderstood?

TWO WHO STAYED

They say that Lot's wife was the bad Jew,
given her chance at salvation not for anything
she'd ever done but only for her husband's piety.
Still, she couldn't follow a simple rule:
keep your head from turning once turned in the right
direction, keep your faith straight and blind.

But have you never opened your eyes during prayer
just to see who else had opened theirs?
When they told you not to look into the sun
didn't you? When they said to shield your eyes
from the welder's torch how could you help but want
the blue flame, if only a moment, blazed into your skull.

This is the story of keyholes and open windows,
forbidden fruit and my son wanting to look
behind the adults only door in the video store.
Or maybe it was more than temptation, more even
than a lack of faith. Maybe some all-too-human grief
cried out from within for that crying out from behind.

There were two daughters, they say, forbidden to flee
by foolish husbands. There was the bed of their birth,
the faces they spoke to every day for years, their place
of worship where they heard the word the first time.
What rough beast in the heart of Lot could not look back
to see those girls gone beyond his favored grace?

What inhuman faith could so displace a father's
love to give them up without a glance thrown back?
What woman's heart would fail to melt
from the heat rising behind her? A pillar of salt—
her tears had already cried that pillar inside
while Lot's face stayed dry and still as stone.

MEADOW: MARY AND JOSEPH

Tired, dead tired, head ringing
with unending questions.
Here, beside this stone,
in the shadow of these trees, lie down.
Rest. I'll kneel beside you and wait.

Who cropped this field, miles
from anywhere? What hand? What foot
cleared this path before us? What
unfathered God lay down this road?
Damned light. Damned voices. Damned city
I go to for this unearthly making.

How alone I feel, and betrayed.
Unwifed, unallowed to do what any man
would do. No child to call my own,
cuckold, outcast, nothing but these
strong-armed angels filling my head,
pushing their happy consequence
of miracles. What do they know
of doubt, shame, emasculation.

To be so chosen, stem of Jesse,
rod of Abraham. Am I reduced
or risen? Father, son, and
holy escort, chauffeur with donkey,
steward to God's great anomaly,
seedless, fruitless bearer of this
living cross. Will I hold him?
Will I cry at his inevitable hanging?
What father will he cry out for?

Unborn prince of unlikely blood,
playing insane games of a Greek god,
what heavenly bliss will this bring me?
Yours is not the only sacrifice
to be made here. What manhood, what life,
what father's hand is severed and replaced?

Sweet, angelic face, near death
in this quiet perfection,
you can't imagine the doubts I've had.
What hands are these to tear and rend?
Some things weigh heavier only because

they have to. How much these eyes

can't see. Rest. Rest. Rest.

MEAT JESUS

There he was, undeniably
outlined in the fat of the first ribeye
I could ever remember having, poor
family, such expense rarely indulged.
The first three were already on
the grill, but my father paused on this one,
perplexed to see familiar eyes gazing
back from a plate puddled with blood.

We all looked, and looking saw,
and later, after the awe wore off,
after the camera and the phone calls,
after debating the definitions
of sin, we drew straws to see
who among us would eat Jesus.

VERONICA'S VEIL

It was his face I wanted to save,
to love into this dull rag, press
to my cheek, wipe clean of dust, sweat,
tears. There was nothing holy in my desire
to have some small piece of heaven
for my own, to hold the strong nose,
full lips, hard, fine features
of a man in the cup of my own hands.

You were there. You saw how perfect
he was, the sores ripe and wet
as bruised fruit, the veins running
like roots beneath his skin.
This face deserved no worms
to consume it, no black hole
of earth to conceal it, no dark
future of creeping up through veins
of lilies, rolling like spitballs
in the intestines of worms, dangling
through fetid waters in rats' teeth.

Look at your own face. Feel the dark
seeds of your eyes, the bright
bulbs of cheek and chin, the stem
of your nose, your lips' soft
petals, stamen teeth, pistil tongue.
Nothing this beautiful, this gentle,
should be torn limb from limb,
should face death on this earth,
bleed in these hands able to save it
only as a leaf dried between two pages.

SAINT SEBASTIAN'S WIDOW

A pious widow found him and nursed him back to health
—Lives of the Saints

I found you, pierced with arrows and left
for dead, hanging by your hands
from a knotted oak, your head pitched
forward, face hidden beneath
the wet rag of your hair. I was old,

had been alone too long, had forgotten
how beautiful a man's chest could be,
the soft thatch of hair, small-boned
ribs pressing against the flesh,
curving around the heart. Even as you

were stretched to snapping, streaked with blood,
I wanted to cup my hands around
your breasts' unopened buds, lay my head
in the pale hollow of your chest,
rise and fall with your breathing.

I cut you down, broke off the arrows,
and struggled to carry you home,
not caring who saw me, what names
they called me. Once there I laid you
in my only bed, dug out the heads,

slowly, like pulling weeds, careful
to displace as little flesh as necessary,
sponging up blood and packing
wounds with my softest cloth.
For days your eyes stayed closed,

head lolling to one side, chest
barely moving. I dripped water
and broth slowly into your mouth.
I offered your body flowers and perfumes,
washed it daily with the best soaps

I could find, lingering over your soft
skin, the limp stem of your loins,
gently fingering each pale curve
of muscle, each ridge of bone.
At night when you moaned with pain,

I rushed to your side, watched your back
swell with air, held your face in my hands,
ran my fingers through your hair.
I wanted to lick the sweat from your brow,
suck the chill from your spine.

I nursed you back to consciousness,
kept you through your weakness,
fed you soup and bones and whatever
meat I could find, and you saying
nothing anyday but "Bless you."

When you started caring for yourself
again, I helped however I could,
enjoying the weight of your body on mine,
your arm thrown across my shoulders.
I knew you'd never stay.

On the first day you left the house,
you walked back to where I found you
and started preaching again.
A crowd gathered, first the people,
then the soldiers. I watched you

from below, only one of many.
Your face filled with glory,
eyes burning with conviction,
chest swelling beneath the robe
I'd made you. I barely understood

your words, but the soldiers knew you,
taunted you, spat at you,
called you ghost, deadman, Christian.
When you turned and swore at them,
condemned them, I saw the anger rise

in their faces. I saw them moving towards you.
I saw how you continued shouting
words like *God, resurrection, salvation.*
I wanted to stop you, to carry you home,
tell them it was only sickness speaking.

I did nothing. I watched them beat you
with clubs until your body was broken,
face bloated with bruises, chest
spattered with blood. I watched them
and cried to see your head give way.

I left you there for someone else
to bury, to chase the rats away,
clean your body, throw dirt across
what I had made so white.
I couldn't save you again. I left

as much alone as I had ever been.
I couldn't undo such ruin,
couldn't cry in your dead hair.
You, your own Sisyphus.
would never be my stone.

THE DREAM OF ST. FRANCIS

It started with the hungry look of stars,
wind a trembling lip, earth
a field of mouths closing on air.
For all I gave I thought that God
would show me the way, give me the means

to make my life a sacrifice.
He gave me nothing but pierced hands,
a dream of the world in need.
All I had left was myself.
I gave my hands to doves, shadow wings

incapable of flight.
I gave my arms to the deep needing
of thorns, feet to blistering sand,
ankles to holes in the ground,
knees to trees crouched in water.

A pair of crows carried my eyes away.
Wrens made nests of my hair.
I gave my tongue to the bleating of sheep,
my ears to bats. A possum wore my scalp
like a helmet. Rats settled in the back

of my skull. I left the skin of my arms
for snakes to inhabit, the rest for deer,
rabbits, raccoons, worms.
The smallest insects drank from the cup of my heart.
Reaching the pond I lay down beside it,

satisfied, unafraid, waiting
for what remained to turn to dust
and ash, for rain to empty this prison
of skin, feed the earth's menu of roots,
castings, runoff to another day.

THE PASSION

Was it the absence of God
that left Joan of Arc
in the fetal position at the stake,
her body thrice-burned
then scattered upon the waters?

She had given all,
life, name, peace
of inconsequence only to be called
madwoman, zealot, witch,
martyr, heretic, bitch.

Cross in her bosom, another
before her, she called to what
causes she could name,
Michael, Catherine, Margaret,
then breathed Jesus at last.

What rightful cause could stand
idly by and watch
youth reduced to ashes,
consumed by a fire that started
long before taking up arms?

THE ANGELS' NIGHT OFF

WHY ANGELS ARE ALWAYS FAT

He took all my pretty ones with him
the ones with tight bellies, long
streaming hair, faces thin as blades,
the ones who had fallen in love
with themselves, and had reason to do so.
He left me only these soft and silent
mounds of flesh, these uninspired,
these bodies needing wings twice
the size you've imagined.

He took all my hungry ones with him,
the ones who ate meat, drank fire,
howled at the moon. He left me
not with shepherds but sheep
fattening on clouds, their wrinkled bodies
growing chins instead of desire.

When I clapped my hands the pretty ones
came slow, always touching themselves
below the waist, lingering to see how
first one, then another thing felt against them.
He never clapped at all, just made his body
like silver, a mirror they'd follow anywhere.

Of course I had to let him go.
That was no way to run a heaven,
everyone looking at him,
myself no longer the center of thought.
But now when I clap, no one comes
at all, not that I wish they would.
Those he left stuff themselves
on dumplings and cream, their bodies
turning to clouds heavy with rain.

Sometimes when he leaves his lights on
I watch them from my high chair.
I like to see the shapes they make
with each other, see their bodies burn
with forbidden fire, see what they remember,
see my face reflected there.

NOW HIRING HOLY ANGELS

Title from a sign on Highway 16 Near Denver, NC

Job Title: Messenger.
Full-time position. No education required.
Duties may include intervention,
retribution, passing through silent rooms,
guarding trees and true believers,
unlocking gates, moving the dead.
Some heavy lifting.

Must have own halo and be willing to relocate,
possess excellent customer service skills,
bedside manner and flair for the dramatic.
Experience with flaming swords a plus.
White robe provided. Prefer blondes
or redheads with long, curly hair.
Fat babies need not apply.

Send name, photo, previous addresses,
age, religion, exact weight,
relevant experience, personal references
and driver's license number for criminal background
check. All applicants will be tested
for drugs, narcissism, and insatiable lust.
Salary: None. Benefits to die for.

EVOLUTION

It starts with your hand floating on water,
your feet leaving no wet spots on the floor.
She was surprised to find how easily she stayed
on top, feeling weightless even on the thin skin
of lake. When she stood up she had to be careful
not to be seen. It's not walking on water exactly
but floating just above the surface of everything.

Waking in the middle of the night you walk
to the mirror and find your entire face
dilated. The past has become a single dream,
more than enough to keep you from sleep.

Already her body yearns for earth,
her feet linger over roots, her hands
try to fly away like leaves, her mouth
leans to kiss every flower she sees.

One day you think you see yourself
disappearing in sunlight, your body scattered
like dust. You move quickly towards shadows.
The strange hair in your back begins to feel
like a feather, your feet curl like talons.

Reaching out to the people she loves
she feels nothing but the light around them.
She no longer knows the imperfections of face,
hand, breast. When she tries to speak
she finds her mouth can only make music.
If she could shed this skin, her body
would burst into flight, her wings cut the sky
like sharp limbs tossed erratic in wind.

THE ARRIVAL OF WINGS

The wings come first—
great fins rising out of your back.
It'll happen when you're alone,
in the hospital room, beneath
the water, your hands busy in bed.

Trying them on, you'll soar
into walls, tangles of trees,
do-si-do in the air, nosedive
to the ground, beat a circle
of bruises about your head.

You'll remark how unlike
the little fat ones you feel.
You'll wonder how they
in their pudge and ignorance
could manage their own so well.

They're just too big really,
and too new. They could enclose you,
if you knew how. They could
lift you to the sky, if you
could find some workable rhythm,

could tame your great flapping,
control your flailing about.
As it is, they only tire you,
lash welts across your back,
beat you half to death.

CLARENCE

When I get to heaven, the old man said,
I expect to hear violins, maybe a cello
or bass, not talking to each other
the way they do in mortal quartets,
but saying with one voice, as tremulous
as the vibration of life itself, "sit back,
relax, put your feet up, enjoy
the view, dinner will be served immediately
by only pretty girls with wings shaped
like violins, but softer, so soft, in fact,
you'll think they could only exist in your mind."

FOR THOSE GROWN TIRED OF ANGELS

Such perfection is boring.
Such unruffled faith impossible,
        not to mention unchallenging,
such permanence uninspiring.

Better to stay this side of human,
uncertain, unclear, imperfect
        and constantly working
towards what you think might last.

THE ANGEL'S SEARCH FOR HEAVEN ON EARTH

In the morning he returns to heaven,
dragging his wings behind him,
his halo loose around his ears.

The night is a bad taste in his mouth,
a memory of retching on doorsteps,
passing out feathers in a bar.

He remembers losing at darts and quarters,
trading small miracles for beer,
swallowing goldfish on a dare.

He remembers tattoos, a rose
on a man's chest, a tiny cross
between his eyes, the pricks in his own

skin. He remembers the taste of sweat
and cigarettes, flaming shots of rum.
He remembers dancing with a girl

named Sylvia, feeling her skin
brushing his chest, touching flesh
he'd nearly forgotten. He remembers walking

in the moon's erotic O, her hands
on his ass, stroking his wings.
He remembers dripping cold water

on her chest, watching the skin shrink,
glisten, stretch, warm to falling.
He remembers her body beside him,

her face a pool of sunshine,
feet painted with raindrops,
crescent moon, starry nights.

He wonders how the world could help
but hold such life, how things like this
are let to fade, pass away.

He can't help but wonder how much
faith he has spread today, how there
could be any wrong in this quiet touching
some small piece of heaven.

MISGUIDED ANGEL

The angel appeared on my table
when my back was turned, garlanded
with pastel ribbons, graceful wings
too small to bear substantial girth,
the miracle of flight peculiar
to heavenly orders, pale alabaster
child's face grinning her beatific
smile, cow eyes forever wide
with surprise, thin finger raised
to her mouth in silent conspiracy
to keep her secret of manifestation.

Exiled from some distant garden
where she should stand scattering
seed for a gathering of birds, squirrels,
wild things made tame beneath her touch,
she peers instead at coffeeshop walls,
offers me a moment's rest
beneath her never-changing gaze,
ultimately, left for some woman
named Joyce who briefly shares her angel
with me, reminded good-naturedly
as she leaves, "Don't forget your angel."

13 WAYS OF ANGELS

1

"It had wings," she said,
her eyes too wide not to be believed.
"It had wings and had Daddy
by the throat." Her mouth wouldn't stop.
"I was afraid to touch him, the way
I'm always afraid to touch him,
the way he always touches me."

2

The first thing he saw
as he ran towards where
the shots came from
was the angelic smile
of the two-year old
reaching up to him
from where she stood
over the sprinkler, diaper
sagging, wrinkled body
glistening with water.

3

Warm sand on my back,
sound of surf sorting the day,
lapping water from your ear and chin,
sucking the salt from your shoulder,
you rise above me,
the moon's halo behind your head.

4

Walking by the hospital I see,
or imagine I see, faces drawn
in every window, eyes uplifted

or closed, mouths shut on empty shells
of words, shadows moving
like uncertain hands on worn out clocks.

5

The angel on my shoulder
is mute as stone and nowhere
near as heavy. In fact, I'd think,
she might have drifted away
if not for the constant smell of cinnamon.

6

Please excuse this spastic flight
of adolescence. 17 years
in the making of this crawdad
body clinging to trees,
stumbling overhead, flying
into nets of hair.
What can you expect for charity?

7

I see them everywhere,
Tooker's paranoiac of the stairway,
haloed head, frightened eyes,
angel afraid of ascent.

8

Cemetery angels with stone wings
hover above the dead,
unable to lift even themselves
from the ground they belong to.

9

When the faces fade
the diabolical chair stands empty,
the sky sits on broad shoulders of trees.
Abandoned by angels
we wait our turn out of the box.

10

Though he looks straight at me
I cannot see the angel's eyes.

11

Moth or angel, muse of my sleep,
humming against the window,
wings beating out dreams until dawn.

12

The angel in the room
is fat and lazy and going nowhere,
Botticellean cherub
insuring only the remote's
batteries live forever.

13

It is always so.
The wind blows against a window
and a light too bright to bear
goes out. All that follows
is a tragedy of crushed petals.

LOOKING FOR FACES IN THE NIGHT SKY

These are things anyone could have made
up. The stars are nothing but stars,
and playing dot-to-dot in the night
sky makes anything possible.
Years ago from the stone porch
my grandfather pointed them out:
the lion, the great bear, the hunter's sword.
This one he called Mary and showed me
how the stars made a woman's face.

Looking for faces in the night sky
we string stars into shapes of things
we fear or long to remember.
I see spider, sparrowhawk, bobwhite.
This one I'll call woman becoming
an angel, the grotesque buds of wings
sprouting in her back.

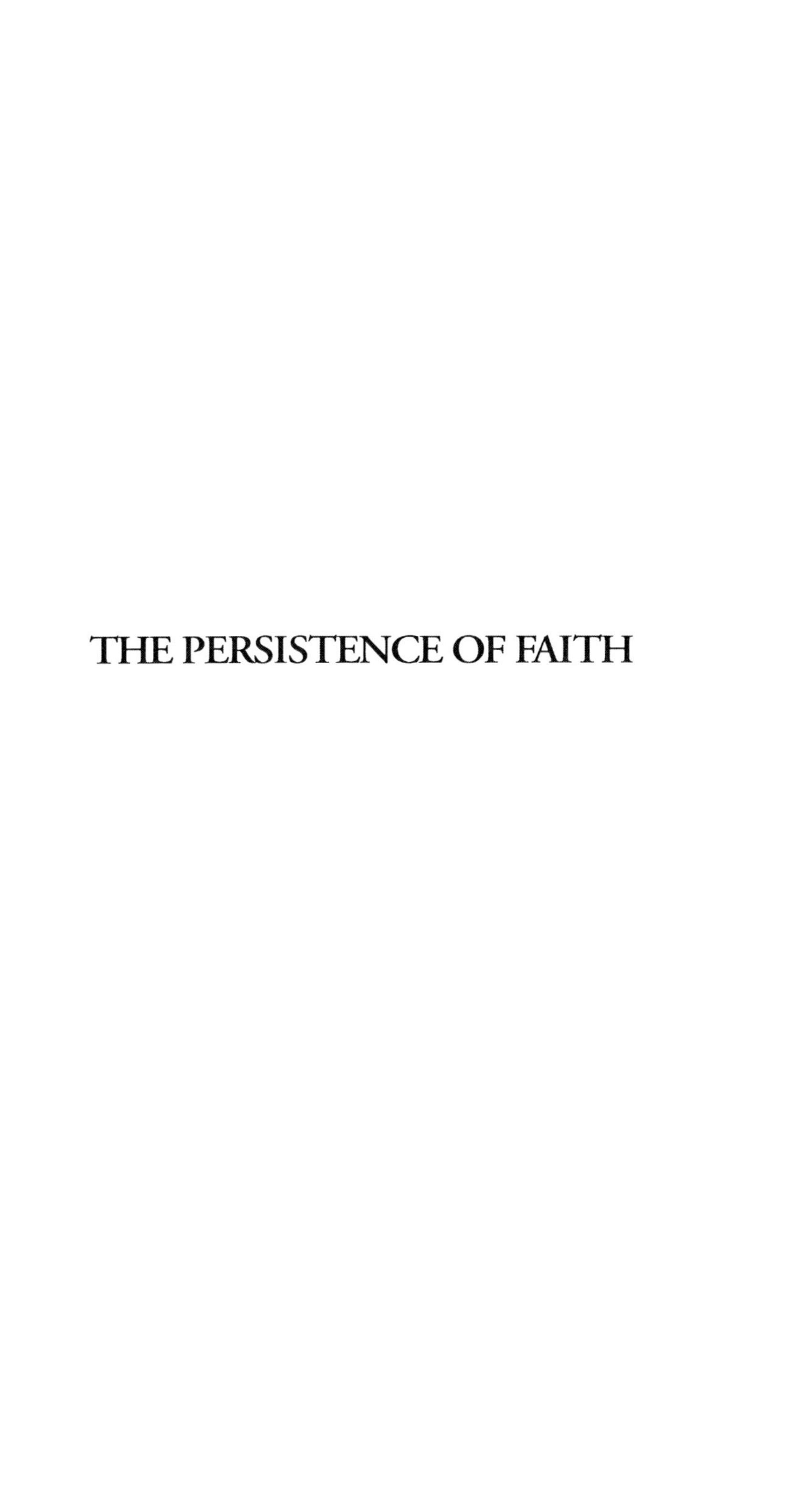

THE PERSISTENCE OF FAITH

FINDING EAST

after Karen Yost's painting Our True Mother

Looking east to the source of everything,
Madonna and half-formed child, all tendon and bone.
What can we make of this disembodied wing?

Our true mother and undeveloped king
stand in half-shell sun, vital features undone,
looking east to the source of everything.

Ursa Major trace of yellow flowers cling
to trees estranged from trunks on a canvas dome.
What can we make of this disembodied wing?

Black fly shadow blocking the road, unfaltering
insect love hummed in ceaseless drone,
looking east to the source of everything.

Childish weathervane compass rose obscurely pointing
scrawled on houseless roof and weathered stone.
What can we make of this disembodied wing?

Deific figure hanging out on the wrong
side of the tree, leaving us nothing but alone,
looking east to the source of everything.
What can we make of this disembodied wing?

IN SPLINTERED VIEW OF GOD

Darkness. Cold.
Head full of black and moaning.
Each shirt a dead child above him
an empty sleeve, an unfulfillment of buttons.
How long he wonders,
this bestiary of boots and walls,
this world behind his right eye,
this mouth closing on darkness.

Sudden light at hinges,
at cracks in the door jamb.
Mystical whistle of movement.
Celestial hum of half-heard voice.
Hands grasp thin ribbons of light.
Face presses to splintered grain of door.
Mouth tongues bits of sound.
Breath held. Heart slowed to match
the pad of footsteps on the other side.

When the footsteps fade,
when the light dissolves to dark again,
he fills the silence with silent
wings of silent things,
faces where the light should be,
with his own mind's screaming for meaning.
He searches the folds of his clothes,
hands, mouth for words, names,
for the "Yes" of an unseen speaker.

PROSPECTING

Beneath the mill,
a red-haired boy,
lies flat on his stomach
stabbed by needles of grass.
He watches reflections twist and turn,
darker shades dissolving at the edges,
a solitary cypress bent on crooked knees
rising out of the water,
distorted clouds floating by,
sails full of wind,
a Jesus bug skating on spindly legs,
the stiff nipple of a coke bottle
peeking above the surface,
the rest severed below.

Lying flat, rippled water seems still,
the rough top of a stone wall,
jagged edge of uncut glass.
He presses flatter,
pulls in his arms and legs
making his body smooth and round,
a stone perfect for skipping
a patient messiah
waiting for water to freeze.

THE STARS ARE FAR AWAY AND BLIND

The stars are far away and blind
not at all the bright eyes
I thought would watch me
while I slept. Walking out,
the moon doesn't follow me
anymore. Its flat surface
is nothing like the mouth
I imagined slipping up
behind me, waiting around corners,
swinging low over trees.

In the half-sleep of just
falling off or just waking up,
the sounds I hear are all
too familiar, all too true,
the cat creaking down
the hallway, limbs scratching
the roof, the house shrinking.

I no longer race to escape
my shadow, making wild leaps
over it, stamping it into the ground,
piling rocks on top of it to hold it
down. I let it follow me
everywhere, sometimes
let it walk in front of me.

DEFICIT

Ain't no sunshine when she's gone.
It's not warm when she's away.
Ain't no sunshine when she's gone
and she's always gone too long
anytime she goes away,
away, away, a way,
not away, a way,
the way, Yahweh some say,
meaning being, meaning I am
all that I am, all that is being,
and some say I say
that every song and poem
is really about god,
about our disappointment in god,
about our distance from god,
meaning we're all suffering
from some huge, life-sized,
lifelong, life-saving
separation anxiety,
meaning we all just want
to get god back in our lives
get back to god
get right with god,
meaning if the song is right
then god just might be a girl
we want to get back
to get god back in our lives
or maybe just to get
to god through the girl
to get to god in the girl
I ought to leave that girl alone.
There ain't no sunshine when she's

IN THE ABSENCE OF ANYTHING AS CERTAIN AS A BURNING BUSH

You look for signs everywhere,
tea leaves, stars, open palms.
You seek out faces in napkins,
clouds, mashed potatoes,
patterns that coalesce into meaning
from stains on floor, ceiling, walls,
that certain array of moles
growing across your knee.
You look for names in spider webs
or skins of apples kept whole in peeling.
You interpret handwriting, dreams,
tone of voice, look for meaning
in scat or the bloody remains of animals,
the exhalations of chinaberry trees,
flight of the great blue heron.
Logic fails; you don't trust feeling,
having lost more than once that way,
and you wonder what intuition is.
You're certain the signs are everywhere,
but you don't know what they are
or worse don't know what they mean.
You wonder what significance
anything could have, cloudburst,
crowsong, even the smallest breath.

SYSTEMS OF BELIEF

after de Goya's *Flight of the Witches*

Faced with such choices—
supplication,
superstition,
miracle by donkey—
I'd cover my head
and run away too.

HOW TO SEE A CRUCIFIX

The arm's shadow drawn longer,
thinner than any arm could be.
Hands like a piano master,
a magician poised to strike
his one trick of resurrection,
like some unformed wings unable
yet to fly. The head down,
the sense of hanging off the cross,
unable to resist a simple law
of gravity. Even this neck bowed
beneath heaven's oppression.

All the things that weren't supposed
to happen already have. A woman
who never fell from grace had grace
fall on her. A child was spared.
A man who forgave everything
was unforgiven.

Why should it be seen as anything
perfect? Holy rapture of sacrifice.
Smile of understanding. Immaculate
cross of body unaffected, arms
unbent, shoulders untwisted.
Flaccid dream of salvation.

You think too much of your own life
to want it this way, to think
this I could bear, to want to be
untouched by the throes of an arm
wrenched alive in pain, the piercing
cry of hands and feet, the body
bent beyond recognition,
beyond the sign of its own name.

THE BOY IN THE CHAIR FINDS CHRIST

After Matthias Grunewald

He knew none of them had it right.
No face in the clouds, etched in the fat
of a ribeye, traced on a can of Budweiser.
No placid beatific shepherd of men
smiling from a cross, sterilized,
wiped clean of blood, sweat, humanity.
No cartoon heavenly host sitting
at the head of the table, surrounded by friends
who flocked to him not for who he was
but for what he was willing to give up,
peace, eternity, the absence of pain.
And then, he saw this,
head askew, arms wrenched
behind him, bent at ungodly angles,
awkward, twitching, skin draped
loose over bone, punctured, emaciated,
fading eyes half-open, unable
to focus, terrible mouth rent
awry in so much pain that nothing
he uttered could be understood.

RETURNING TO THE FATHER

Returning to the father,
the son, the ghost
of years behind him,
draws close, touches
the chest to feel
the constant rise
and fall, touches
the mouth to feel
the moisture he hardly
remembers, touches
the eyes webbed
closed with sleep,
the face a pool
on the pillow,
the hand cool
and wet with sweat.

All these things
he remembers
like photographs
left in the past,
a man in love
with mountains,
naming birds
he hadn't seen
before, a man
in love with water,
with ducking and rising
wet with laughter,
a man whose hands
could only touch
with the distant
comfort of play.

How may rocks,
how many trees
has he touched
softer than this
flesh. How many
wild things has he
stroked with more
ease than this
father. Son, ghost
of inhibition
before him, stands
a step away, keeps
a safe space between
them, a space charged
with wings, landslides,
moistness of mouths.

A BRIEF READING FROM THE HOL(E)Y BIBLE FOR SELECTIVE HOMOPHOBIC CHRISTIAN FRIENDS

Select, *You shall not lie with a male as with a woman.*
Unselect, *Nor shall you put on a garment made of two different materials.*
Declare it irrelevant

Select, *If a man lies with a man as with a woman,*
both of them have committed an abomination.
Unselect, *You shall not round off the hair on your temples*
or mar the edges of your beard.
Proclaim it obsolete

Unselect, *The camel, the rock badger, the hare, the pig*
of their fleshes you shall not eat.
Dismiss as immaterial.

Unselect, *Anything in the seas or the streams that does not have fins*
and scales, they are detestable to you
and detestable they shall remain.
Deem apocryphal.

Select, *Love each other as I have loved you;*
If I have all faith, so as to remove mountains,
but do not have love, I am nothing;
God is love, and those who abide in love, abide in God.
Select, but simply ignore.

ART OF WAR

I have delivered Jericho into your hands, along with its king
and its fighting men. March around the city once
with all the armed men. Do this for six days.
—Joshua 6:2

The sound of marching is heard once again
in the ancient streets of Jericho.
—NPR Report, 14 Nov. 2007

You'd think they'd have it down by now,
the marching, the men, boys really,
standing in lines, four deep,
in squads of a hundred or so,
lining up on the right shoulder
of the one in front of them, arms length
apart. You'd think after 3000 years
of forming rank and file in Jericho,
Cairo, Jerusalem, they'd be experts,
soldiering genetically encoded
or handed down like words some 800 generations.
You'd think thousands of years
of civilization would be enough
to make practice unneeded,
the art of war second nature at worst.

THE RIGHT ONE

Suddenly, there was the right one.
Where there had been confusion,
now the choice was clear.
Everyone knew it was the right one
because it said so.

Men cried. Women swooned.
Children did what children do,
singing songs about the right one.

Almost at once there were right one t-shirts
and hats, right one shoes and jackets.
There were bumper stickers that said
The Right One Saves; The Right One
is Lord: The Right One Is My Co-Pilot.

Before long the right one was catching on
everywhere. Monks in Tibet
chanted hymns about the right one.
The great tribes of Africa danced
around the right one's shining altar.
The Russians welcomed the right one
with open arms. All the great poets
wrote great poems called "The Right One."

Eventually the right one was all that mattered.
People gave their lives to the right one.
They knew the right one would save the world.
They made it their mission to bring the right one
to those who didn't have it. Governments ruled
by the words of the right one. Those opposed
to the right one were strung up, crucified
chased from one town to another.

Those who remained tried everything to be
like the right one. They stripped themselves bare,
ran naked through the streets. They abstained
from everything except the right one.
They tore their flesh, fasted, sacrificed
themselves until at last there was only one,
the right one.

REFUSING GRACE

He doesn't count the days anymore
or the times the man comes down,
loosens the straps enough to let
him eat and drink. When it's over,
when the man withdraws, he seems
hardly a man at all, whimpering,
fumbling pants and apologies,
stumbling up the stairs. The boy
no longer cries, no longer fights
or screams obscenities. He mostly
keeps his eyes closed, hoping
to remember as little as he can.
He hears the man upstairs
afterwards, falling to his knees,
Holy Jesus! Mother Mary!
The boy is twelve. He knows enough
about God to know he isn't here
and never will be.
He knows enough to hate this
Christ who presumes to forgive,
this man who presumes to ask.

ABSOLUTE VALUE

He wanted to understand
absolute value, thought
that might mean the redemption
of everything, hookers and addicts,
his own life, thought
that might be what Jesus
meant, *enemy as brother,*
each other as I you,
judge not that you be
not judged, but no matter how
he tried, understanding,
forgiveness, silver linings,
things kept coming up the same,
always less than zero.

USING MY NAME IN VAIN

Murder, slaughter, genocide, rape,
bomb, gun, bullet, hate,
acceptable loss, collateral damage,
casualty, deterrent, torture.

Don't worry about *shit, piss,*
fuck, cock, cunt, balls,
cocksucker, motherfucker, goddamn it all
to hell when the hammer hits the thumb.

All the words are my name.
Forget Yahweh, Jehovah, Christ,
Elohim, Adonai. None of them
come close. None of them possibly could.

But *bitch* I can do without.
Nigger, chink, raghead, heretic,
faggot, blasphemer, slut, whore—
all in vain
            all to no end
                        but destruction.

DAY OF ATONEMENT

Why ask where none can answer?
If God lives, surely it is in the trees
beyond the bimah, in the earth
incorruptible from which they grew.

If God breathes, his breath is the invisible
wind that moves all things
in a constant dance of turning.

If God exists, surely he is in the child
whose joy knows no limit of time or place.
Repent the scorn you cast upon his voice.

How can the sound of a child offend you?

On this day three nooses still hang
from a tree in Louisiana.

On this day the bodies pile up,
the losses running ahead
of the memory of loss.

Somewhere on a road I can never
get back to is a woman I wronged,
a child I failed, a man whose hands
I can never forgive. My sins gather
around me unshriven. The day turns.
So much remains unsaid.
I will never stand here alone.

On this day they removed the child,
the father put up token resistance,
and the spirit went out of the place.

PERSISTENCE OF DOUBT

I want to say there's a reason the hawk's tail
is the same red as pine needles in November.
I want to say his hornet's nest body in bare trees
means that someone is watching.

I want to say the kingfisher's blue splashing
back to water shows how everything returns
to what it came from, the brown fingers of rivers
wrapping around everything I know shows that something
holds us close to the earth we're born to.
I want to say that blackbirds streaming out of treetops
proves that heaven and earth share their ways of turning.

But the wind rushes by me like a voice
whispered through a wall, a lesson too close
to be unheard, too far to be understood.

And the past gathers behind me like nightfall,
and the night grows wider with every mile,
with every minute gone by, and the distance between me
and where I was and the place I want to be
and tomorrow,

I can't imagine what it will be like,
and tomorrow,
I must let go of it today,
and tomorrow,
how could you hold such a thing on your tongue?

THROUGH THE VALLEY OF THE SHADOW

After a photograph by Joey Bowman

Though I walk through abandoned mills
littered with plastic milk jugs, fast food
wrappers, 2-liter bottles full of piss,

though I walk through busted open
crack houses with flattened mattresses,
plastic bags, the ash of little fires,

though I walk through hotels
with rooms by the hour and see
the tousled beds and spent condoms,

though I walk beneath trestles and bridges
with lumber laid across rails,
cardboard standing between abutments,

though I walk through dew-wet tents
made of sheets thrown over low branches
and filled with leafmeal for warmth,

though I walk through Sunday parks
and see the men covered with newspaper
breathing cold smoke from empty mouths,

though I walk I will fear no thing
but the nothing that surrounds us all.

TRAJECTORY

White bodies rise like miracles
from the ground, their angles of ascent
inconsistent, determined perhaps
by destination, the way the arc
of a basketball depends upon
the distance it's asked to travel.
The souls they carry believe
in the means of science to overcome
such rules as gravity or death.
I've seen the big headlights
lined up, leaving Charlotte
one by one as if the way to heaven
were as simple as persistence.

STEWARDS

Is it possible such wildness lives
only here?
Whale calf and whale,
green islands in a blue sea,
mountains like old men,
flocks of birds darkening the sky,
the annual enflaming of trees.
What unforeseeing god
would make it so?
What reckless will
to put all in one basket?
And what lack of wisdom
to appoint one
with such willingness to waste?

THE PERSISTENCE OF FAITH

Some things he knows are true,
the night, the sound of rain rising,
then falling, heavy, then lighter,
on the roof, on the steps outside,
the light of the Christmas star
swinging in the doorway, in the wind,
the shapes of cars sliding down
lit streets in the night, the lights
of windows left on for someone
not sleeping, someone not there.

Some things he can only imagine,
the wind, the leaves like footsteps
at the door, the limbs brushing the sky's
dust of clouds, the drivers
of cars almost lost in the night,
in the rain, the destinations,
the faces waiting in the windows,
the stars like the eyes of God.

THE SENSUAL WORLD

after Sam Tallman's photograph "Mountain Dawn"

Twin worlds of sky and lake,
mountain and trees,
even this low-lying peninsula
finds reflection here,
jagged edge repeated above
and below.

Cleft of trees and rock,
gentle pinnacle, red sky
burning up the black,
evergreen leaning towards
water, all things pulled toward
a single point of plausibility.

A place I've been
and long to be again,
a time that seems
to come every day
but can never be quite
the same.

One could get lost here,
unknowing real
from reflection
and walk out into water
seeking what fire burns
below.

IN THE CATHEDRAL OF FALLEN TREES

Each time he thinks something special
will happen, he'll see the sky resting
on bent backs of trees, he'll find
the wind hiding in hands of leaves,

he'll read some secret love scratched
in the skin of a tree just fallen.
Because he found that trees were not
forever, that even trees he knew

grew recklessly towards falling,
he gave in to wisteria's plan
to glorify the dead. He sat down
beneath the arches of limbs reaching

over him, felt the light spread
through stained glass windows of leaves,
saw every stump as a silent altar,
each branch a pulpit's tongue.

He did not expect the hawk to be here.
He had no design to find the meaning
of wild ginger, to see leaves soaked
with slime trails of things just past.

He thought only to listen
to the persistent breathing of trees,
to quiet whispers of leaves in wind,
secrets written in storied rings.

Each time he thinks something special
will happen. He returns with a handful
of dirt, a stone shaped like a bowl,
a small tree growing rootbound against a larger.

COMMON GROUND

My brother has never kept a single lake,
a single lost grave to himself.
Always he calls, then waits until I
can come, lets me lead the way,
find it like the first time,
shouting the names I know, the shapes
of bird and stone, cloud and tree.

Once in the same day I saw
a kestrel, a mantis, an arrowhead
and took it as a sign, though since
I have seen each in their own days
and miles away from each other.

I do not believe God will bend
to kiss this mouth. I do not believe
the wine will turn to blood. But something
knows the moment of sunflower,
the time of crow's open wing,
the span of moss growing on rock,
and water washing it away.

In the pictures I remember, there is you
letting me stand on the fallen tree
as if it were mine. There is you
letting my arm rest on top of yours
around our mother. There is you
lifting me up to the limb I couldn't reach.

This is the faith I've wanted, to know
that even now we are capable of such
sacrifice, such willingness to love.

NAMING

Little Sawyer, I hold you swaying
through Shabbat—your tiny body
pressed against my chest, listening
to hymns in words I do not know—
vowel words, like yours, all sibilants
and liquids, a gentler tongue than mine.

Your body translates this spirit
like all you've already taught me:
the meaning of perspective, the reality
of clichés—apple of my eye,
greatest joy, answer to prayers
I had all but ceased to say.

I know I've never been this strong before,
can only hope I'll hold this joy,
this sense of being something bigger:
your brothers, your mother and I, Little Sawyer,
whom we'll call Eliana. I know now
that God has answered me.

THE SENSE OF PLACE

Nothing happened here.
No one was born.
No one died.
No one fell in
or out of love.
An unexceptional child
was raised here
in the room with mustard yellow
walls unlike any
seen elsewhere because
two people rolled on
one layer of custom-made colors
after another for 20 years.
It is enough that the room
could hold a family comfortably,
that candles on the mantle were burned
down to almost nothing
from lighting every Friday night,
that sunlight, filtered through leaves
of a weeping cherry, poured in
through large front windows
each afternoon making
the room warm and bright
even on the coldest of days.
It was enough that three doors,
each marked with mezuzah,
welcomed anyone in or
opened on anywhere you wanted to go.

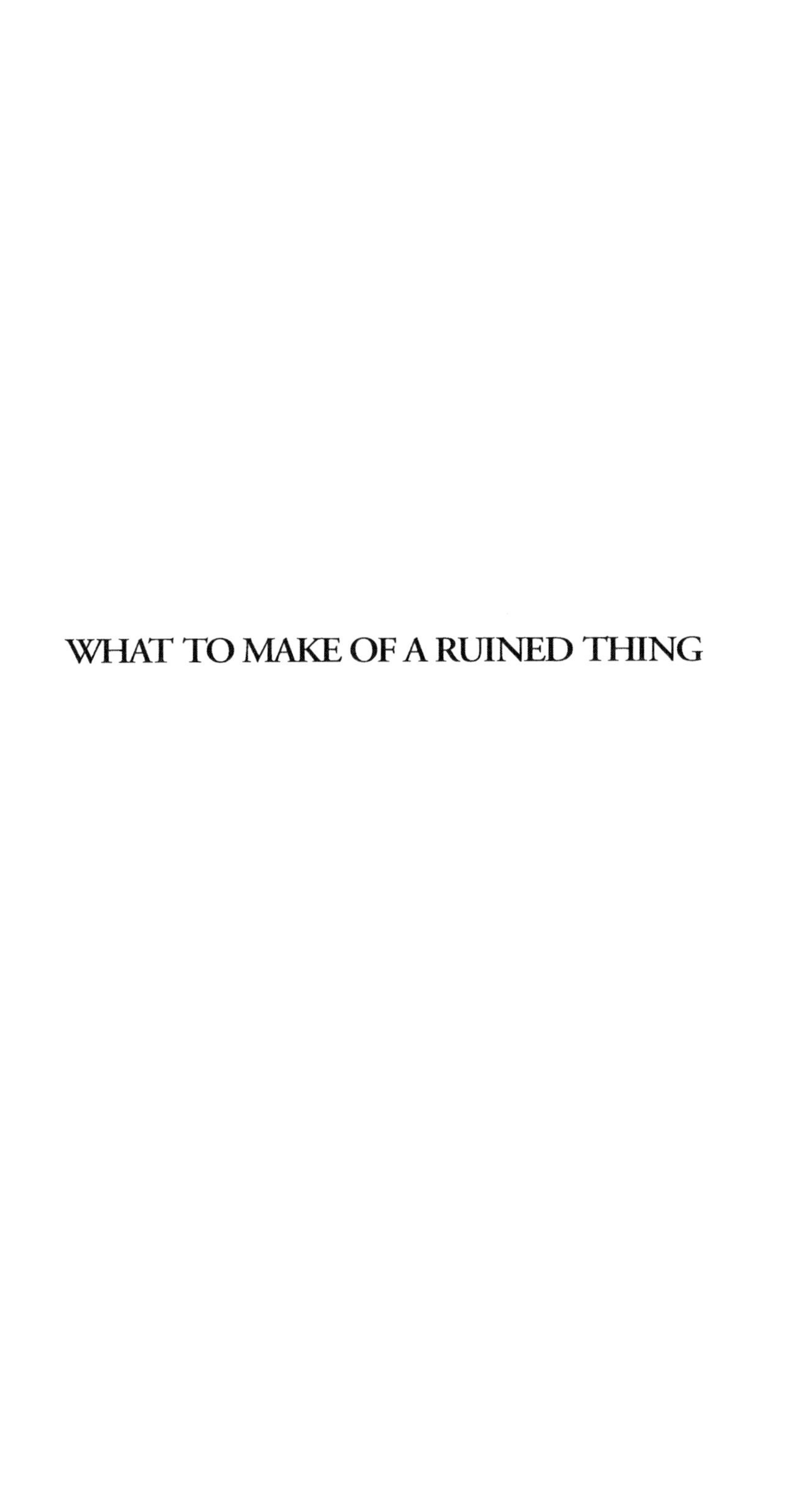

WHAT TO MAKE OF A RUINED THING

who spoke of him
have died
making him extinct

ON THE ISLAND OF MISFIT TOYS

On he Island of Misfit Toys
all the rooms are full
of trains with square wheels,
planes afraid of heights,
inflatable dartboards, balls
gone flat, polka-dotted elephants
and birds that swim, animals
unstuffed, missing
arms, legs, eyes.

The Bumbles Ballroom hosts
a convention of occupationally-
challenged dentists, oversized
elves, poets who teach.

The restaurants can't keep up,
serving blind ambition,
unrequited desire, foolish
hope, various forms
of lubrication night and day.

Only the beaches are abandoned,
sand strewn with human
hearts, broken and still.

And God, having already used
fire, famine, flood,
collision with asteroid,
sits alone in the hotel's
business center imagining
the possibilities of negative
space, trying to ignore
the flutter of his eyelid, constant
twitch of his tired right hand.

THE DYING COST OF RISING

after Jonathan K. Rice's "The Rising Cost of Dying"

Why not ascend early and avoid
the rush—Armageddon's crowded
gate? Inflate your ego to lifting;
be spirit, soul, vesper,
ether, air, mist, prayer
uplifted like hands or surrender.
Deny gravity; inhale helium.
Leap from high places. Think
yourself as light as air. Avoid
regret, guilt, the concept of sin,
anything remotely heavy. Erase
any sense of self, hope of satisfaction.
With enough practice you too
can rise without awaiting rapture.

NEARING THE END OF MY SENTENCE

I grow desperate for more
meaning, more time.
I grope about for a preposition,
conjunction, participle.
I lack justification for another phrase,
through the gossamer backlit dress,
notice the modifiers are drying up,
the silhouette of bare thighs,
have too little time for adverbs,
her legs wrap hungrily around my waist.
I wonder what comes next,
descending towards oblivion,
how painful the transition might be.
I long for a semi-colon, a dash,
at least another comma.

THE JOURNEY

You start with unspeakable excitement,
anticipation of what might be seen.
You stand in line with countless others,
some exchanging stories of times past,
rumors of what is yet to come,
most simply silent, uncertain,
still afraid of being in the wrong
place, of missing the boat, of judgment.
Pull of tide, squawk and flap
of ubiquitous birds, groan of rope
around capstan. Of course there are sights
and sounds, long-legged birds along the shore,
blast of the horn, an occasional dolphin,
flute of wind in your ear, the uncommon
gannet, but for most the waiting itself
is delicious, the real stuff of life.
Everything else becomes routine.
At the other end, nothing,
a ferryman, an abandoned island, angels
with mosquito wings, bored with heat.

POST MORTEM

Maybe we all get to the place we believe.
Good Christians sit on cloudy thrones,
strumming harps, preening wings,
spinning star fragments at those
less faithful than themselves. Bad ones
sit on thorns, turn on roasting spits,
scream against their own minds'
hellish inventions. Hindus come back.
Buddhists achieve Nirvana. Atheists
lie in the ground and rot.
Heroes are carried off to Valhalla's
lofty halls. Pagans cross the river,
the bridge, descend into Hades,
fly up into the sky, join their gods
in paradise. New Agers take off
for distant stars. Some few stay,
transparent and scary, rattling
chains, searching for lost heads.
Ultimately, all turn bone to coral
and plank, eyes to pearl and stamen.

Imagine each arriving at their personal doorways
to heaven, some Valkyrie with St. Peter's face
clutching the keys, checking doom's black book,
asking which heaven you envisioned.

I know a good place to go
to be dead, body or soul,
music or flight, terror of stars
falling, dust and stone, ghosts
of barbed-wire fences, the garden
of your son or daughter—
a green planet, not too yellow
yet, full of the warm rollings
of earthworms, always ready for return.

GOD TALKS TO THE DEAD

He tells them not to worry,
tries to reassure.
He says there's a plan,
that everything he made
is already redeemed. He says,
how could it be otherwise?
He tells them just try
to forget about the living.

He acknowledges he never foresaw
the making of meaning, strength
of attachment, endurance of sorrow.
God talks to the dead
to tell them he's sorry
he couldn't do better than this.

AFTER LIFE

What a sick, demented fuck God must be
to want to sit and watch the watching
they are bound to do, sisters, husbands, children
left behind, wanting, needing, struggling
for meaning or breath, unknowing
what comes next or how to get there.
Or else to brainwash, demand amnesia
for what they spent a lifetime creating.
He so loved the earth that he gave
his only begotten son? Gave how exactly?
Brought him back to be with him, beyond
suffering or death or uncertainty, the incomplete
made whole again, a trick disallowed the other
residents of heaven, the so-called happy dead.

THE SYNTAX OF THINGS

When I die
I want to be dead,
a clean conclusion,
no lingering ambitions,
thoughts of continuance,
no sitting on clouds
filled with knowledge
of God, self-satisfied,
watching the living,
unblissfully uncertain,
for death is nothing
if just another paragraph,
and life is less
if only parentheses.

LAYING DOWN THE TRACKS

He thought he'd find the way
to God there, head down
across the tracks, listening
for what might come from anyplace
but here, for what might lead
to where the answers are found.

What brought him here is hard to say
and doesn't really matter, boredom,
loss, disappointment, a sense
of going nowhere too long with too much
effort and no sign of relief.
He thought the rest might be nice.

Instead, he felt the press
of gravel against his face,
the night growing colder,
smelled the stench of pine pitch
until he couldn't take it anymore,
rose and walked away.

Three times more he found himself
on such a narrow path,
on rooftop, hillside, and then behind
the wheel. Always he left
just short of his destination
never knowing the miracle of his own salvation.

LEAP OF FAITH

You know it can be terrible
here, what with bombs
and Norman and children dying,
and just the idea of
cockroaches outliving us all.

You've lost your faith in goodness,
and the leap, you say, could be
exhilarating,
but
that leap is also a leap of faith
that things will be better
somewhere else, life
without pain or loss,
rest, sleep.

But in sleep there are dreams,
and in dreams there are nightmares,
and no one can really know.
There may be nothing. There may
be Dante with his black book
and implacable rings.
There may be less.

Here at least there is ice cream
and poetry, there are flowers
and the ever-opening sky,
there are faces and the occasional laugh,
there is gravity and the still
certain orbit of moons.

RESISTANCE

When the hand comes to rest
on my shoulder, I won't turn around,
or smile, or open my arms to it.
I won't willingly rise,
death's easy trick of levitation,
from the table laid out before me,
some meat I've prepared, some
prepared by others, the drink
poured by all who came before.

I'll finish the meal, savor the last
drop of wine and ask for more.
I'll argue the time is not right,
a mistake has been made. I'll call
names, scream embarrassing insults,
then dig fingers into the underside
of the chair, clamp teeth on anything
that comes near, slam my head
against their chin, the bridge of their nose.

Strong-armed angels, four at least,
will grip beneath each arm
and leg, pry at fingers
untwist feet from legs of chair,
and I'll use my words again to beg,
cajole, sing them into submission
for just one more second,
as if I had something
worth fighting to the death.

INVERSE OF FIRST

Most firsts we won't remember,
shock of air hitting our lungs
at first breath, assault against
the eyes at first sight, the exact
point at which we become. And yet,
we might know them by inversion,
the panicked gasp when wind is knocked
away, the urgent grasp
for definition when the lights go out,
the solemn cessation when the switch is turned,
uncertain swimming towards something else.

INSTRUCTIONS AT THE GATE

Empty Pockets.
Discard jewelry, belts, umbrellas.
Remove shoes, hats, coats,
any articles of clothing with sentimental value.
Take off glasses. Vision returns to perfect.
Pull out IVs, ventilators, feeding tubes, catheters.
Implants will dissolve as new tissue grows.
All blood will be washed.
Scrub away tattoos.
Urinate. Defecate. Retch.
Shed any remnant of mortal consumption.
Wipe hunger from the buds of your tongue,
pleasure from the palette.
Forget what seemed to matter:
desire, ambition, possession, love, sources of fear.
Close your eyes. Breathe deeply.
Expect a little sting as memory is wiped clean.
Let go of the world.
Step forward.
Behold the nothing of all, void of unencumbrance.
Do not look back.
Pass.

MITIGATION

Jihadi decapitation,
Bolshevik dismemberment of hands
to keep the buried alive
from digging their way out,
Nazi conversion of skin
to lampshades, Nanjing, My Lai,
Hiroshima, Murambi, Darfur,
Matthew Shepard, James Byrd, John McGraham.

I watch my wife stroke
my daughter's hair in fevered sleep.
A much too simple solution,
nonetheless persistent and true.
All the atrocities of man
assauged by this hand, this hair.

in the presence of
not there but here
what could be greater